Allie the alpaca

Written and illustrated by Mia Cuneo

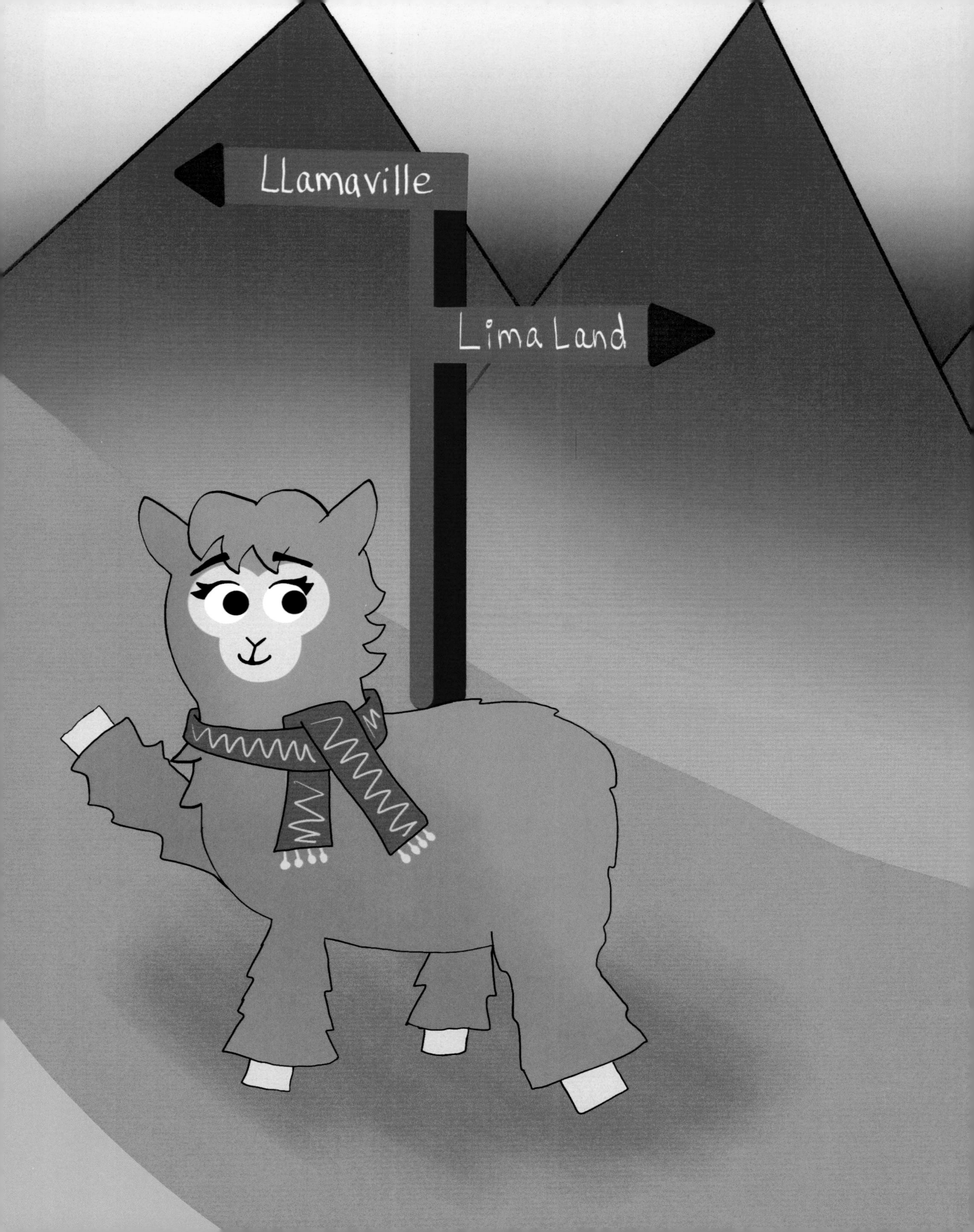
LLamaville
Lima Land

Allie the alpaca was excited to start the day. She was going to a brand new school, but her old friends were far away.

She trotted up the school steps,
and opened up the door.
She met a cheerful smile
from her teacher Mrs. Fleur.

Mrs. Fleur brought Allie to the front of the class...

But when she was introduced,
she thought she heard a laugh!

Another llama asked,
"Allie, why are you so small?
Did you not grow enough?
When will you get tall?"

The entire class were llamas,
Mrs. Fleur included.
Allie never felt so low,
never so secluded.

Allie looked at the laughing crowd and stretched to her fullest height. She said, "I'm an alpaca, not a llama, get that right!"

"But it's what is on the inside that counts," Allie said with pride.

I hope my new classmates understand, and all this teasing comes to an end."

The whole class clapped their hooves, the bad moment now passed.